# One and Universal

# One and Universal

## Prayers and Meditations from Around the World

*Edited by* John Midgley

SKINNER HOUSE BOOKS

BOSTON

*Printed in Canada.*

Cover design by Suzanne Morgan
Text design by Sandra Rigney

ISBN 1-55896-427-4

Library of Congress Cataloging-in-Publication Data

One and universal: prayers and meditations from around the world / edited by John Midgley.
     p. cm.
   ISBN 1-55896-427-4 (alk. paper)
    1. Unitarian Universalist churches—Prayer-books and devotions—English. I. Midgley, John, 1939–

BX9855.O54 2002
242'.809132—dc21                                                    2002017918

10 9 8 7 6 5 4 3 2 1
06 05 04 03 02

*Editorial note.* In some parts of the world, religious expression remains entirely masculine. In order to respect this and avoid any impression of cultural imperialism or the imposition of uniformity, such material has been left largely unedited. In some cases, a few gentle adaptations are noted in brackets.

We gratefully acknowledge use of the following:

"The Woman of Samaria" from *Aotearoa Psalms* by Joy Cowley. Reprinted by permission of Catholic Supplies Limited.

"Not by Compulsion" from *Seasons of the Soul* by Robert T. Weston.

"Sing!" by Maury Merkin. Copyright © Maury R. Merkin. All rights reserved. Reprinted by permission of the author.

"Carol Our Christmas." Words: Shirley Erena Murray ©1992 Hope Publishing Co., Carol Stream, IL 60188. All rights reserved. Used by permission.

Every effort has been made to trace the owner(s) of copyrighted material. We regret any omission and will, upon written notice, make the necessary correction(s) in subsequent printings.

# Contents

Introduction                                                      vii

## Celebrating Life

Opening Words                    *Canada*              3
Not by Compulsion                *United States*       4
Sing!                            *United States*       6
On Change                        *Spain*               7
Carol Our Christmas              *New Zealand*         9
Prologue                         *Sri Lanka*          11
Fertile Word                     *Sri Lanka*          12
Meditation                       *Sri Lanka*          13
The Glory of the Outward World   *United Kingdom*     15
A Song for the North             *Canada*             16
Epilogue                         *United States*      18
Winter                           *Canada*             19
Increasing Our Awareness         *New Zealand*        22
Today and Each Day               *Romania*            25

## Communion with the Highest

The Web of Life                  *United States*      29
A New Year Meditation            *Czech Republic*     31
Remember, O Seeker               *United Kingdom*     32
Surrounded by Mystery            *United Kingdom*     33

| | | |
|---|---|---|
| God with Us | *Romania* | 34 |
| Call to Worship | *Romania* | 36 |
| In Times of Success and Failure | *Philippines* | 37 |
| A Prayer of Faith | *Madras, India* | 38 |
| Opening of Worship | *Khasi Hills, India* | 39 |
| Hymn | *Khasi Hills, India* | 40 |
| Closing of Worship | *Khasi Hills, India* | 41 |
| Longing for Prayer | *Hungary* | 42 |
| Speak to Us | *Hungary* | 44 |
| Make Us Stilled | *Northern Ireland* | 46 |
| Time of New Birth | *Northern Ireland* | 47 |
| The Woman of Samaria | *New Zealand* | 48 |

## Living in Harmony

| | | |
|---|---|---|
| The Fields of Promise | *Canada* | 53 |
| Fruits | *Hungary* | 54 |
| Strong and Free | *South Africa* | 56 |
| In Times of Conflict | *Philippines* | 58 |
| The Song of the Afflicted | *Philippines* | 59 |
| We Gather in Your Name | *Pakistan* | 61 |
| The Flame of Light | *Pakistan* | 62 |
| Light and Warmth | *Pakistan* | 63 |
| On Extinguishing the Candle | *Pakistan* | 64 |
| Boldness and Redemption | *Khasi Hills, India* | 65 |

One World—A Litany of Celebration *United Kingdom*    66

Love, Unity, and Peace    *Pakistan*    68

Infinite Spirit of Life    *United Kingdom*    69

The Ground in Which We Sow    *United Kingdom*    71

Remembrance    *United Kingdom*    73

Prayer for an Interfaith Gathering    *Nigeria*    75

To Live Means to Live Together    *Germany*    76

We Believe    *Denmark*    78

Longing for Harmony    *Czech Republic*    79

Roads    *New Zealand*    80

About the International Council of Unitarians and Universalists    81

Notes on Contributors    85

# Introduction

Throughout the world today, Unitarian and Universalist churches, congregations, and organizations vary enormously. Some have a long history, usually rooted in the Judeo-Christian tradition. Others have had a shorter life, and still others have emerged out of indigenous roots. In order to serve this worldwide network of Unitarians, Universalists, and Unitarian Universalists, the International Council of Unitarians and Universalists (ICUU) was established in 1995. Offering a range of services that include personal visits, publications, and leadership seminars, the ICUU, through its constitution, affirms the belief in religious community based on liberty of conscience, the inherent worth and dignity of every person, justice, compassion, responsible stewardship of the earth's living system, and commitment to democratic principles.

In this small volume readers will discover the rich diversity of worship styles represented in the ICUU membership. Some of this diversity may surprise those whose experience of Unitarian Universalism is limited to their own group or culture. Beneath the variety collected here lies an impulse towards a free religion that serves the Infinite Spirit of Life. My hope is that readers, though separated by geography, history, or experience, will come to feel that they are part of something One and Universal. While many ICUU member groups are located in parts of the world where religious freedom permits an open expression of faith, others are located in countries where worship is severely restricted. The ICUU is committed to the belief that matters of the spirit can transcend political boundaries.

Throughout this volume, we have indicated the country of origin for each piece. Because the Khasi Hills and Madras regions of India present distinct brands of Unitarianism, we have made an exception to the rule and indicated these areas specifically rather than as simply from India.

I extend warm thanks to the Council of ICUU for inviting me to undertake this project, to Mary Benard of the Unitarian Universalist Association for helpful editorial suggestions, to Clifford Reed and others for support and practical assistance, and to my wife Celia for continued help and encouragement.

John Midgley

# Celebrating Life

# Opening Words

We light this chalice to remind ourselves of that flame which
   burns in each of our hearts.
Remembering that when flame meets flame,
   match meets candle,
   the two become one,
   belonging to each other.
Many flames join together to form the warmth of community,
   of congregation, of city, of nation.
We gather here together to remind ourselves of our inner lights
   and join with others to light the way to a good world
   community.
But before we can shine a light on that path, we must remind
   ourselves who we are,
   and we must know who we are.

We are Unitarians, Universalists, Canadians, friends, visitors,
   seekers.
Let us worship together.

Joan Montagnes
*Canada*

# Not by Compulsion

Let us dare to believe in the future;
A future when people shall have learned to live by freedom
And not by compulsion,
By love and not by fear,
By adventure and not by jealously guarded security.
They shall live in peace and shared respect
And "none shall make them afraid."
They shall be continuously hungry for knowledge,
And none shall say it is forbidden them;
They shall live in trust, and none shall do them hurt.
They shall explore without fear of what they may find,
And the difficulties they meet shall be the stepping-stones upward.
Though this be slow in coming,
Though it appears that all this may never be universally shared,
It will be open to all on the condition that each chooses individually.
None shall create barriers between a person and the fulfilment of the
     human spirit
Which the person may not alone overthrow.
It is the barrier we build against others
Which holds us, ourselves, back;
The defenses we painstakingly establish
Become our own fetters.
This could be the future of humanity if we dare:

The people seek to master themselves instead of others,
And rejoice in the fruits of disciplines
They choose for themselves.

Robert T. Weston
*United States*

# Sing!

Sing!
If not forever, through the night;
If not together then alone;
If not in tune then with a hearty sound
But sing.

Or hum.
If all the words can't be recalled,
Syllables will do;
Or pluck upon an instrument.
The meter matters too.
Enliven it with pulse
And hum.

Then dance
If you can find it in your heart to.
Use a step you've used before
Or learn a new one.
More's the better.
Abandon comes in handy,
Prance!
It's Life Time.

Maury Merkin
*United States*

# On Change

Change is not easy. Sometimes we long for things to be predictable. But our experience is that things actually change.

Every day we have to face new possibilities. There are new variables that we must take into account. Some changes are completely unexpected, because we have been blind to the events that were happening around us.

Even we change, as persons. Sometimes suddenly, when some event has had a profound effect upon us: a death in the family perhaps, a new job, or a new awareness about ourselves that allows us to see our life in a new way.

But more often we change subtly. We hardly notice it. We only realize later, when we look back to the path we have followed in our life, or when we meet an old acquaintance who suddenly says, "Hey, you've changed a lot! You look different."

This, then, is for sure; change happens; and there is no single way to deal with it.

So what are our expectations about change? Do we welcome it? Very often change is viewed as a threat. We feel uneasy, insecure about what is going to happen. And very often things turn out well, sooner or later.

Let ours be a religion that deals with change, evolution, and new developments. Let us learn of Process Theology, thoughts of mathematician and philosopher Alfred North Whitehead. He believed that all the universe is in permanent change, in process.

He believed that even God changes.

But how does this change occur, according to Process Theology? Whitehead wrote...

> ...there is a creative tendency in the universe to produce worthwhile things, and moments come when we can work with this tendency and it can work through us. This creative principle is everywhere. It is a continuing process. Insofar as you partake of this creative process, you partake of the divine....

There is nothing to be afraid of. If we accept the idea that the universe is creative, and that change produces valuable things, we will welcome this change with wonder and happiness, knowing that by doing so, we are in harmony with something that is greater than ourselves.

Jaume de Marcos
*Spain*

# Carol Our Christmas

Carol our Christmas,
    an upside down Christmas;
snow is not falling and
    trees are not bare.
Carol the summer, and
    welcome the Christ Child,
warm in our sunshine and
    sweetness of air.

Sing of the gold and the
    green and the sparkle,
water and river and lure
    of the beach.
Sing in the happiness
    of open spaces,
sing a nativity summer
    can reach!

Shepherds and musterers
    move over hillsides,
finding, not angels,
    but sheep to be shorn;
wise ones make journeys
    whatever the season,
searching for signs of the
    truth to be born.

Right side up Christmas belongs
        to the universe,
made in the moment
        a woman gives birth;
hope is the Jesus gift,
        love is the offering,
everywhere, anywhere,
        here on the earth.

Shirley Murray
*New Zealand*

*tune:* "Reversi"

# Prologue

Rain clouds, sunbeams,
star clusters that lasso round the moon
Are linked in friendly concord.
Fowls of the air, and earthbound creatures,
ponds and lakes and fish that
brave the mighty ocean and joust in joy;
Trees and vines that provide fruit
for the sustenance of human and beast
in our home of health which enriches life—
All these are the multiform facets
Of that supreme message delivered silently.

We are the children of mother earth.
Human creatures and beasts form the soul of the earth.
Our earth—the habitat of love.

We are gathered here today
To reflect on how nature sheds fragrance
For our lukewarm souls.
Day and night we bear the weight of our struggles
As burdens,
And gather here now, to seek their resolution.

Walter Jayawardene
*Sri Lanka*

# Fertile Word

Mother earth is the temple
that links humanity and our creator;
Her altar is lit by food and floral offerings;
Holy water and solemn symphonies
Spring from the earth.

We come out of our mother's womb;
The infant sucks sustenance from the earth
and gains strength and vitality.
We who have sprung from the creator
And through nature—
Are a product of that rational ordering
and have prospered immensely.

O God, if strength, order, and justice are your attributes,
We pray now—again and again,
For that power
Which we sorely need, now.

We need that fertile word,
And the resultant blossoming,
In our struggle for existence.

Walter Jayawardene
*Sri Lanka*

# Meditation

Be silent, make your mind calm and
maintain it unruffled
You are the handiwork of mother earth.

Consider your contribution for the
betterment of humanity.

As you came out of your mother's womb
you commenced to inhale the air
from the atmosphere
you learned to produce sounds.
You learned from the gentle breeze, the rain, and those
sounds uttered by birds and animals;
from the words spoken by your parents.

You learned to speak.

You were nourished on your mother's milk
Which had its origin
In the fertility sucked from the
produce of the earth.
And so,
The love we confer upon earth
Springs from our deep affection to our mother.

Human life is
the product of divine creation;
Divinity is the blend of truth and justice.

Walter Jayawardene

*Sri Lanka*

# The Glory of the Outward World

O God, we thank thee for this universe which is our home: for its grandeur and its beauty, and for the abundance of life which covers the earth. We praise thee for the overarching sky and for the driving clouds, for the winds of heaven and for the constellations on high. We praise thee for the salt sea and the running waters, for the everlasting hills and the quiet valleys, for the trees of the wood and the grass beneath our feet. We thank thee for our senses by which we can see the splendour of the morning, and hear the jubilant songs of birds, and enjoy the fragrance of the springtime. Grant us, we praise thee, a heart wide open to all this joy and beauty; and save our souls from being so absorbed in care or so darkened by selfishness that we pass heedless and unseeing, when even the thornbush by the wayside is aflame with the glory of God.

James Martineau
*United Kingdom*

# A Song for the North

Most of us live here in the city;
cars, noise, haste, movement,
blurring colours into grays and compact browns,
pressing time into capsules that work.
Some of us live in a slightly greener world;
rows of cornfields and soybeans,
perhaps a cedar swamp,
the call of a loon on a lake.
But still the frequent crossings of roads and tracks and the
      abutment of fields
        are there to tell us that we are in a world constrained by
        our own creations.
We live, as one once said, like a bead of toothpaste
squeezed out along the border;
      a neat line of commerce, habitations, and intense relationships.
But unlike our friends to the south, sandwiched, rather than
      squeezed,
we know that while we face south so often, behind us is the expanse;
tundra, icy blue glaciers, muskeg, space,
an unimaginable silence,
rocks of ancient rivers clicking together with the movement of time,
and land so open and free that no man or woman has ever seen it.
Though we live constrained and pressured lives,
we know there is a place where time stands still, where the air is fresh
      and crisp and

moves as a single gust across unbroken land,
where sounds are only muffled by distance,
and we know that it is always there, behind us, as we look south.

Joan Montagnes
*Canada*

# Epilogue

Now is the time to live; now is the time,
As nature may disclose, to savour life:
To know its streams, its woodland hills to climb,
To read its cliffs, engraved with ancient lore,
To share its moods, the carefree and sublime,
And thrill with beauty from its ancient store.

Now is the time in wonder to explore
From whispering tree and soft ans'ring dove
To storied shells beside the storm-swept shore,
From starflower to galaxies above:
Then shall peace flood the restless heart once more
As Autumn beauty fills the woods we love.

Now is the time to live, to look to see,
And taste that life is good, to share its zest
And know its patience in the dormant tree,
The budding earth, the motion that is rest;
Creation in each moment flowing free
Nor dread the sunset in the dark'ning west.

Robert T. Weston
*United States*

# Winter

Let this be a time and place
where we not only inquire about life,
discuss its elusive purposes,
wonder about the meaning of ourselves,
or the fraught destiny of our times;

Let it also be a place where
we accept ourselves,
our times and conditions.

Let us learn to live with what we are,
before we rehearse what we might become.

We accept the snow of winter.
It lies about us like immortality.
We learn to see its beauty in the dance of its falling,
in the strangeness of its clinging,
in the even silence on the level land, in the sixfold
        pattern of its smallest flake.
We see it reddened with frosty sun
and streaked with purple shadows.
We learnt to frolic on its slopes
or lie within its limitations.

We accept the winter of ourselves.
But even so, hemmed in by immobility,

we learn how much we contain.
Fallow, we wait the germination.

We accept the contours of the earth
and its degrading forces.
pressure of many seasons' snow, grind of glaciers,
and the tumbling havoc of melting water;
they have worn down the eminences
to lay a carpet of common earth.

We accept the starkness of the earth.
Serac, crevasse and conical contortion,
peculiarly we are carved.

We accept incongruity.
The pompous and the placed,
the down-at-heel and smartly groomed,
the amazing variety of us,
we chortle at Adam's brood.

We accept what we cannot assimilate.
The tardiness of truth,
magnanimity too slow unmelting,
justice congealed in winter's discontent,
this is the grain of us.

But when the reckoning shall be made
we know that more than ten can be
counted good
in the city of destruction.
The hand of wrath is stayed.

Leonard Mason
*Canada*

# Increasing Our Awareness

Those present may call upon the spirit within them or the spiritual powers beyond them to increase their awareness. May each of us be "in tune with the universe."

There is so much in this life that we take for granted.

Let us today become more aware of those things for which we should never cease to be thankful.


We are here, together, like-minded people, arriving after different journeys, ready to respect and learn from each other, ready to search together for the meaning of our puzzling lives—indeed for the great puzzle and wonder of life itself.

Our journey is not ended, but we now take it together in companionship. As we travel, may we grow in wisdom and as spiritual people. Let us be aware of the great miracle that our different paths have led us to discover each other.


May we at all times be aware of those in our affluent society who suffer hardship and injustice—and may we support all human efforts to build a caring society.

May we be a compassionate people, and our first rule: be kind.


Here, in a remote corner of remote islands, at the very edge of world society—a world itself only a tiny speck in a vast universe—here we meet again and meditate, and wonder and give thanks together. Here we enjoy the amenities with which generations of the human race have endowed us. Here, we can communicate in moments with those we love in very distant places. In a few years, by human ingenuity, our world has shrunk. May our efforts seek to break down the spiritual differences and spread love and mutual tolerance.

Let us never cease to be grateful to those who pioneered the way and cheerfully accepted great hardships and all who in any way improve the quality of life and especially for those who lessen suffering not only for ourselves but for all living creatures. Let us be thankful for all healers of mind and body and soul.

Here in this quiet, bright little town, we have so much that we must never take for granted. May our times together quicken our awareness of our very special blessings in what must be one of the loveliest areas of our lovely planet Earth. Here, in our fertile plain, where food and flowers grow in abundance, we enjoy the variety of the scenes around us—the inspiration of hills and mountains, sparkling rivers, wonderful seascapes, and the kindest of climates. May we be of those who cherish the earth.

Let us be aware of the wonder of our own minds and bodies and senses through which we perceive all the wonder; aware of human artifacts from distant ages and many places; of all the vast treasures of history and fiction, poetry and song.

Let Us Wake Up, and Be Aware.

Elspeth R. Vallance
*New Zealand*

# Today and Each Day

O God,

Be with me each new day as I wake.

Whatever I have to face, be it joy or sorrow, give me strength to carry through the new day. Give me to know that when I arise in the morning I must give thanks for the morning light, for life and strength. I must give thanks for my food and for the joy of living.

Give me hope—in doing your will.

May the warmth of the fellowship we have shared this morning be with us through this coming week. May we draw strength from the faith we hold. May we prove our faith by extending our love and tolerance to those whose ideas and values may be different from ours. And may we find strength in humility, courage in adversity, joy in diversity, and a true sense of purpose in our prayers.

As the deer pants for cooling streams, we too seek the clear waters of life.

And so, in the coming week, may our ears be open to tidings of joy and gladness. May there not arise in the heart of anyone, envy of us; nor in us, envy of anyone.

O God of mercy and love, bless and prosper the work of our hands,

for our life,
and for your kingdom.
Amen.

Miklos Székely
*Romania*

# Communion with the Highest

# The Web of Life

There is a living web that runs through us
To all the universe,
Linking us each with each and through all life
On to the distant stars.
Each knows a little corner of the world, and lives
As if this were the all.
We no more see the farther reaches of the threads
Than we see of the future, yet they're there.
Touch but one thread, no matter which;
The thoughtful eye may trace to distant lands,
Its form a continuing strand, yet lose all its filaments as
    they reach out,
But find at last it coming back to the place
    from which it led.
We move as in a fog, aware of self
But only dimly conscious of the rest
As they are close to us in sight or feeling.
New objects loom up for a time, fade in and out;
Then, sometimes, as we look on unawares, the fog lifts
And there's the web in shimmering beauty,
Reaching past all horizons. We catch our breath,
Stretch out our eager hands, and then

In comes the fog again, and we go on,
Feeling a little foolish, doubting what we had seen.
The hands were right. The web is real.
Our folly is that we so soon forget.

Robert T. Weston
*United States*

# A New Year Meditation
## (Following the Death of Norbert Capek in Dachau)

We reach again for the plough to turn the furrow anew. There is unknown soil in front of us, maybe full of stones, roots, and thistles, dry and poor.

It will be necessary to seize the plough with strong hands, to place it deep into the soil, with concentrated power and attention toward all obstacles we may encounter on the path.

Nothing will discourage us from going into the struggle against all obstacles, because we believe that You will be with us, and You will empower us in this work which brings pearls of sweat to our foreheads, with which the thirsty soil will be watered.

We believe that not even the greatest of difficulties will cause us to break down and abandon our goal. However great the effort and however great the trouble, there is trust in Your help.

We believe that we need not fall down onto that hard, rocky soil, even when we feel deep tiredness, for You can refresh us with the gentle wind and the moist air, and invigorate us further toward new efforts to make the fallow earth fertile.

We believe that from the seed we sow in the ploughed soil, good young corn will grow, and our work will not be in vain. For You will bless our endeavours with success.

Karel Haspl
*Czech Republic*

# Remember, O Seeker

Remember, O seeker,
This truth divine,
The Light is within thee,
Let the Light shine!

John Andrew Storey
*United Kingdom*

# Surrounded by Mystery

We are surrounded by mystery
        but not darkness;
Uncertainty, but not defeat.
We are surrounded by love
for which we may reach out
        in any time of need
And give again to those who need us.

Sheila Crosskey
*United Kingdom*

# God with Us

Our eternal and providential God,

In the spirit of prayer and repentance, we are conscious of our human pettiness and we search for you. We seek you because we believe, and we know that you are of the greatest worth and you are the greatest treasure in our earthly life.

For all that we are and all that we have we owe gratitude only to you. The fullness of our life is in your hands.

We arise from you through the mysterious reality of birth, just as the daybreak arises with the sun; and we will return to you and rest in you, just as the daylight disappears in the darkness of the night.

In the experience of prayer we have often felt the quieting of our inward storms. We have discovered that a more highly ordered world of love is opened to us. We have felt that we are partaking of the higher spiritual life of the soul, beyond our material lives.

From among all your creatures you have favoured us with spiritual life and knowledge, and the desire to seek the best and most beautiful in our earthly lives, in order to create a home of peace and love for all the peoples of the world.

We strive for this highly ordered ideal world, but frequently we wish to escape from the risks involved; frequently we are not victorious in the face of temptation and evil; our limbs are weak and our will is not strong.

But our spirits are filled with desire to discover love toward God and to our neighbours. As human beings, in our everyday struggles, we have felt distant from our real purpose, distant from a world of love.

We live today in hard, difficult times, filled with worries, troubles, struggles, and wars. Yet peoples and nations are looking toward the future with hopefulness. We human beings cannot know what tomorrow will bring to us, but we believe that you, our loving God, will be with us and will bless any noble thoughts and truthful actions.

We pray to you, our providential God, that your help will be with us, through our knowledge and talents, which we have received from you, that we may be able to serve a peaceful, love-filled future for humanity.

Amen.

György Andrási
*Romania*

# Call to Worship

O God,

who is not far from any one of us, but nearer and more present to our souls than are our own bodies, grant us the spirit of prayer, which is the key that can unlock the Kingdom of Heaven within us, and admit us to all that is good, beautiful, joyful, and worthy.

Teach us day by day to love You with all our hearts, with all our soul, with all our mind and all our strength.

Teach us day by day to love our neighbours as ourselves and to serve one another in Love. Let love be the strong link between person and person, between nation and nation, between religion and religion. May we believe in the glory of Love on the earth, which is our home.

Help us to live by faith; give us love to show our faith by our works, that those we meet may honour Your providence which never fails. In all we do, and in all our work, make us seemly, diligent, worthy.

May we never forget the kindness that surrounds us in the present, nor be careless of treasures we have inherited from the past, but having a lively sense of our debt to our brothers and sisters, and a loving remembrance of departed generations, may we reverently carry forward the work of the ages, and daily endeavour, as faithful stewards, to enrich the same by a good conversation and a holy life.

Elek Rezi
*Romania*

# In Times of Success and Failure

Great God,
Help us to have faith that neither success nor failure will
   separate us from your love.
In our success, cause us to understand that what we achieve, we
   could lose.
In our failure, make us to perceive that tomorrow is a new day,
      and give us a humble heart to appreciate those days that
      are yet
   to come.
Promise us that your requirements are a clean conscience, a
      loving spirit, and a forgiving heart.
Amen.

Pere Carl Q. Sienes
*Philippines*

# A Prayer of Faith

Our loving and living God, I kneel before thy throne of grace and offer my sincere thanks for all the good that you are pleased to bestow upon me in this world.

I praise thee with gratitude, to express how blessed I feel to receive your care and concern in my life, all the time.

Grant unto me the necessary wisdom that others might know that I am your child forever. Help me to serve you, master, as your loyal servant by my thought, word, and deed, and thereby remain a blessed soul in this vast universe and also be a blessing to all around in my daily living.

Show me the right path, to follow in your footsteps. Keep me always safe, to walk aright and to draw closer to your mighty presence in times of need.

Pour on me showers of blessings. Give me courage to face evils and overcome them at all times. I need your power to love my neighbours, and my enemies as well.

I crave your tender mercy to help our leaders in my motherland, to uphold the everlasting peace that you have assured mankind on this globe.

All these I place before thy mercy seat, with reverence and faith.

Unitarian Church Congregation
*Madras, India*

adapted

# Opening of Worship

O God we thank you for the opportunity to attend this act of worship. Let us be attentive, and direct our thoughts to the hymns, readings, prayers, and all our spoken words, so that we may live a life that is filled with goodness. Let us feel your presence in us always.

Amen.

Anonymous
*Khasi Hills, India*

adapted

# Hymn

There is no one greater than God,
Today as in days of old;
On high and low, he still governs,
Within and without, he discerns;
He is with us, he is with us,
With us ever and ever.

There is one God, one righteousness
And one true religion;
To love our God and love our friends
Everywhere, is our watchword.
He is with us, he is with us,
With us ever and ever.

God is our true Father and Mother,
Human beings are his children,
Both men and women are one family,
Rich and poor his children.
He is with us, he is with us,
With us ever and ever.

Hajom Kissor Singh
*Khasi Hills, India*

adapted

# Closing of Worship

O God, we thank you before we close this service. Let all truths we have heard abide in us so that our lives may be worth living; and let us feel your presence in us for ever and ever. Amen.

Anonymous
*Khasi Hills, India*

adapted

# Longing for Prayer

Our all-providing God,

At this moment we long for prayer, peace, joy, sanctification, now that we stand before you. Often there are great walls, strong barriers, obstacles blocking the way, and it becomes impossible for us to achieve our desires. That is why we suffer so much, we feel anxious, we feel ourselves thrown upon life's mercy. If we understood that longing for prayer, wishing for it, already means prayer, we would be happier.

The lungs need fresh air; the heart needs fresh, oxygenated blood. In the same way, we need to meet you in our souls, to meet you in truth, on both holy days and weekdays.

Our other self, that stays behind, is the human being of the weekdays, with its tempers, its selfishness, hardness and roughness. But the self that stands in front of you now, wants not only to be more joyful, but also much better, cleaner, more understanding, more generous and true.

Our wish for rebirth, to be different, becomes a torturing thirst. We beg for your nearness that cleanses us, sanctifies us, elevating our souls.

That is why we read the Book of Books, the Book of Life, the Scripture, the Book of Good News, "The Home Pharmacy of Mankind" as Goethe called the Gospel. We read it to enable darkness and sadness to vanish from our souls.

The Gospel, the good message, is always young, even though we often feel old. Even if we have not gathered many years, we often feel old because we do not understand the truth of the Gospel's contents.

Prayer means closeness to God, leading to everlasting youth. This is the beginning of Christian self-consciousness. This is why we pray to You now, just as, long ago, the disciples asked the Master, "Please, teach us how to pray."

Jozsef K. Kaszoni
*Hungary*

# Speak to Us

Eternal God,

Once You chose to speak to your people through your prophets, and now You address us also. You address all those who are able to hear, understand, and grasp in their conscience, Your heavenly message. You address us through eternal laws, and we approach you now with the word of prayer.

Our voice seems as a gentle breeze, Yours is often a resounding tempest.

Our word is weak and obscure, Yours is pure wisdom.

Our words mean always our requests, Yours—eternal law.

In spite of all of these, we pray that You accept the weak bubble of our tongue.

Today we want to worship your perfection in our words. Let them express our gratitude for Your blessings. But since to be human means also to be perpetually asking of You, may our words express again our requests.

What should we ask of You this time?

Should we ask for bread to nourish our bodies?

Should we ask for clothes, to protect us and keep us warm?

Should we ask for good luck, good health, and strength to be always with us?

Thousands of wishes are released when we unlock the door of our wishes. But today we do not ask for all of these, but only for one thing. That we may believe—and this will include all these other things.

Speak to us with teaching words when we are tired: "Come to me, all who are weary and heavy, and I will give you rest."

Speak to us words of comfort when we cry: "Blessed are those who mourn, for they shall be comforted."

Speak to us words of wisdom when we feel tempted: "But resist him, firm in your faith...."

Enlighten our minds and strengthen our will, so that we can accept all these sayings as pure truth, and help us to believe in them as valid for our whole lives.

Amen.

Jozsef K. Kaszoni
*Hungary*

# Make Us Stilled

O living Spirit within us all,
Speak to us in silence,
In the silence of the crowd,
The silence of our inner echoes.

Holy Spirit, help us to pour out what good within us lies,
Whether it be silent exchange with other souls,
Or taking another's hand and holding it;
Knowing it is your will.

Ever-present Spirit,
Convert our isolation into relationships,
And our relationships into everlasting ties that bring
Peace and beauty.

Remain in us unstilled,
Until you make us stilled.

Angus M. McCormick
*Northern Ireland*

# Time of New Birth

Come Emmanuel:
Disperse our darkness with your light;
Dispel our insensitivity with your compassion;
Diffuse our selfishness with your justice.

Come Emmanuel;
Come, forgive our insensitivity;
Come, plant our seeds of love.

Come Emmanuel;
Come to our world;
Come to our Church;
Keep coming into our lives,
To change and transform and renew.

Come, Emmanuel;
God with us in the mystery of a humble birth.
Keep on coming, Emmanuel,
Today and always.

Christina Jones
*Northern Ireland*

adapted

# The Woman of Samaria

I know a woman of Samaria
(Samaria is everywhere these days)
who went daily to draw water from the well,
and who heard that Jesus was coming
to the well on a certain day,
especially to see her.

The woman sent him a message:
"Master, this is a very great honour!
I am overwhelmed by your kindness!
This well is a busy place
but I shall be here all day
with a banquet prepared in your honour."

When the morning arrived, she was ready,
and, as usual, the place was busy.
Over three hundred people came to the well that day.
Some of them looked at the banquet hungrily,
but she chased them away
and kept watch for her special visitor.
He didn't arrive.
There was no sign of him all day.

Disappointed, and a little angry,
she sent him another message:

"Master, what happened to you?
You said you were coming to visit me at the well."

And Jesus sent a message back to her:
"I did. I was there more than three hundred times."

The women thought deeply on this,
then wrote to him again:
"Dear Jesus, please, in the future,
when you come to see me.
will you tell me who you are?"

I don't think she got an answer
to that one.

Joy Cowley
New Zealand

# Living in Harmony

# The Fields of Promise

What we are we have reached because of other people's planting. The thoughts, the values, the ideas, and the feelings we possess are articulate because we have been the recipients of knowledge, kindness, love, and understanding. And above all, the Mystery we call Life we owe to a presence yet unknown yet still very near to us. For these gifts not our own, we give thanks.

And now, may we have the faith in life to do wise planting, that the generations to come may reap ever more abundantly than we. May we be reminded of the wise ones of old who admonished, "If you plan for one year, plant grain; if you plan for ten years, plant trees; if you plan for centuries, plant souls." May we be bold in bringing to fruition the golden dreams of human kinship and justice. This we ask that the fields of promise become fields of reality.

V. Emil Gudmundson
*Canada*

# Fruits

The fruit of quietness is prayer;
The fruit of prayer is faith;
The fruit of faith is Love;
The fruit of Love is service;
The fruit of service is peace.
—Mother Theresa

Eternal Spirit, in whom we live, move, and exist;

Here and now, everything around us inspires quietness, peace, and harmony, inviting us to prayer. This means nothing other than a conversation with You, a meeting with You, and sanctification in You, our God. So,

The fruit of quietness is prayer. And there is a great need for prayer in this world full of discord, where our deeds and feelings are aggressive. The noise of big towns hinders all of those who keep looking for You. Violence, anger, nervousness seem to rule the world! But when we pray, our prayer always gives birth to its fruit, that is, nothing other than faith. That is why we can utter with Mother Theresa...

The fruit of prayer is faith. And when we have faith, we are not uncertain anymore, we do not feel ourselves at everybody's mercy, because we know that You exist and we exist, and we do not feel lonely in this fearfully vast universe. Faith in its turn gives birth to its own fruit, and Mother Theresa says...

The fruit of faith is love. Not only do we know that, "God is love, and they who abide in love abide in God and God in them," but we also feel the miraculous power of love. And since, according to the teachings of Jesus, "You will be recognized when you love one another"—we know we are nothing without love. When we bear in our hearts active and forgiving love, everything around us seems to change at once. The lives of those who believe in Love, and accept its rules, receive a new meaning and aim and mission. Thus . . .

The fruit of Love is service. Those who are able to understand this sequence of ideas, those who have tasted these fruits, are also able to serve. They are able to serve in the ways the apostle taught, in good and bad times alike. There is always enough to do, there is always much to harvest. But the harvesters, the labourers, the service bearers are few. That is why there is always a need for those who want and are able to carry on in service, even if it brings sacrifice and exhaustion. In this way, service gives birth to its fruit and . . .

The fruit of service is peace. And it is in peace that everything unfolds, achieves its purpose. It is only in peace that we can move from one step to another, from the small to the great, from the physical to the spiritual. That is why, in the sequence of prayer, faith, love, and service, we pray for peace in our souls.

Amen.

Jozsef K. Kaszoni
*Hungary*

# Strong and Free

Grant Us the Grace to be United, Strong and Free

Look down with mercy on our native land:
Wild, untamed forests, wastes of burning sand.
Mountains that raise their rugged crags on high,
Rivers that thirst for rains that pass them by.

Give us the breadth of vision like our plains,
Where the deep silence of thy presence reigns;
And, with the vision, grant us clearer sight
To move through darkness to the dawn of light.

Teach us the peace that lives in veldt and vlei,
That to our fellow pilgrims on life's way
We may bring comfort, courage, joy, and rest.
In sharing burdens all of us are blest.

Then, in thy love, keep safe from every harm
Dwellers in village, town, and lonely farm.
May we Thine Image in our neighbour see:
Beyond all pride of race, a unity.

Strong in thy strength, and loving tender, true,
As we take up the work that each can do,
In this great country, by thy grace, may we
Stand up united, purposeful and free.

Robert Steyn
*South Africa*

# In Times of Conflict

God of Love,
You have called and bound us together into one, common life.

Help us.
> In the midst of our diverse relations as we struggle for justice and truth, that we may confront one another without hatred and bitterness,
> And have eyes open for opportunities for mutual patience and respect so that we may embrace new horizons.

Touch our bruised feelings, comfort our broken hearts, and calm our shattered minds,
> that we may reconcile the broken and the tormented,
> reunite the detached and the fractured,
> through your gracious name.
> Amen.

Pere Carl Q. Sienes
*Philippines*

# The Song of the Afflicted

Is there a God?
In a world of injustice and inequality?
    of oppression and tyranny?
    of poverty and ignorance?

God, where are you?

I know of a kind, loving, and gracious God
Who is honest, just, and fair.
Whoever, whatever, and wherever you are
Hear my cries, my pains, my agonies.

God, where are you?

Hear the calls of the people who are in a fractured society.
Their calls are true, genuine, and real.
They are hungry for justice and equality,
They are thirsty for real love and happiness.

Do you hear me, please?

Hear me, O God.
Listen to me now
And act on my behalf, now.

Gracious, loving, just God,
Now is my time.
Amen.

Rebecca Q. Sienes
*Philippines*

# We Gather in Your Name

O God our creator, we gather in your name and we light this candle in your name,

    You are a loving spirit,

    Bring and place your love in the flame of our enlightenment,

    So that its heat and light may transmit your love and peace among us and make us to be at one with you and with all humanity.

    Amen.

Samina Tufail Gill
*Pakistan*

# The Flame of Light

O God, as the flame of light brings light and warmth to us, we pray that this same light and warmth may penetrate our hearts and minds and take away all darkness and coldness of doubts, and make us tolerant and patient, so that oneness can be generated among us, your children.

Amen.

Samina Tufail Gill
*Pakistan*

# Light and Warmth

O God, as this candle brings light and warmth by burning itself, may we sacrifice ourselves to bring light and love and the warmth of compassion and sympathy to all. May all human minds and hearts be at one with you and with all human beings.

Amen.

Samina Tufail Gill
*Pakistan*

# On Extinguishing the Candle

O God, as we now extinguish this candle we ask you to keep the light and warmth in our hearts and minds, so that we may amend our thoughts, words, and deeds and be at one with you and with all humanity.

Amen.

Samina Tufail Gill
*Pakistan*

# Boldness and Redemption

O God, root and source of body and soul,
we ask for boldness in confronting the
evils and tribulation that beset us.
With you within us, we have the power
to outface all that is troublesome and
untrue.
Mother and Father of all humankind,
we redeem our failings by the good
work that we do. In the name of the one,
the only God.
Amen.

Anonymous
*Khasi Hills, India*

adapted

# One World—A Litany of Celebration

*Leader:* Let us celebrate the unity of the world,
the reality beneath our divisive illusions,
the vision that lifts our eyes to the
future that could be.

*Congregation:* May there be an end to a world order
based on distrust and enmity, which
violates the human temples of the
divine with exploitation and idolatry.

*Leader:* Let us celebrate the glorious diversity of
the human race, the infinite variations on
a single theme.

*Congregation:* May there be an end to injustice and prejudice;
to all that persecutes
and diminishes people because of what they
are and what they believe.

*Leader:* Let us celebrate the web of life that enfolds
this good earth,
rejoicing in its beauty and variety.

*Congregation:* May there be an end to all that
despoils and destroys this global
home of ours; may we and all people
discover our oneness with the Universe.

*Leader:* Let us celebrate the resources of the earth and
give thanks for them, for the life and
comfort and pleasure that they give us.

*Congregation:* May we work for an end to the hunger,
the poverty, the despair that arises
from the wasteful husbandry and selfish
disposal of humanity's inheritance.

*Leader:* Let us celebrate the divine Spirit
at work among us and within us—kindling
the love that knows no bounds, that
enfolds our one world and reaches out
into eternity.

*Congregation:* May the Spirit clear our sight,
inform our minds and touch our
hearts. May the one-world vision
be ours; may we dream it,
pray it, live it.

*Leader:* Let us celebrate our unity here together.
May what is true for us now be true for
more people everywhere until the whole
world knows that it is one.

Clifford M. Reed
*United Kingdom*

# Love, Unity, and Peace

O God of life, we come to your refuge.
We pray to you.
As you have made the earth to give crops,
The sun to give light and heat, moon and stars for guidance, and the
    same air to breathe for all human beings, we pray that you will
    shower the blessing of love and unity for all humanity.

O God, as you have created the same eyes for human beings to see
    with,
The same ears to hear,
The same nose to smell, the same tongue to speak,
The same mouths to eat, the same blood to circulate in the human
    body,
We pray that you will grant your blessing to all human minds and
    hearts,
So that minds may think and hearts beat for love, unity, and peace.

O God, grant to us all life, health, happiness, and wisdom,
And bind us together in this life and the life to come.
Bless the ones who do wickedness to us,
Have mercy on the ones who are dishonest and bad to us.
Bless all of them, and bless us as we continue on our way to love,
    peace, and unity.

Samina Tufail Gill
*Pakistan*

# Infinite Spirit of Life

Infinite Spirit of Life, we would serve you
and all humanity. We would
strengthen our worldwide faith for
this purpose, rich as it is in the variety
of its living traditions.

We seek to build religious community.

We would found it on liberty of conscience
and thought; on belief in the inherent
worth and dignity of everyone.

We dedicate ourselves to justice and
compassion, to responsible stewardship
of the living earth, to the democratic
process in ordering our human affairs.

Fostering and strengthening each other
as members of one family,
humbly sharing what we have found with
others who might benefit from it,
we would live out our common values
for the world's good.

May we respond to the human condition in
ways that reflect the faith we profess.

Infinite Spirit of Life
one and universal;
around us, among us, within us;
we would serve you and the
whole human community.
Awaken and strengthen us to do so.

Clifford M. Reed
*United Kingdom*

# The Ground in Which We Sow

As sowers we go out to sow,
to sow the seed of our liberal faith.

But we are conscious that the ground in which
we sow can vary from place to place.

For some, the hard, stony ground of the
secularized society.
For some, the fertile ground of people
seeking refuge from regressive religion.
For some, the unbroken ground where our seed
is new and the task is to just get rooted at all.

Some face the choking weeds of religious and
political hostility; others are plagued by
parasitic growths that sap their strength.

Everywhere the ground is different, but the
seed we sow is resilient. It has survived and
thrived in many fields. It has sprouted anew
where once it was uprooted and trampled.

For our seed to flourish it must adapt to new
environments, changing climates; it must have
an inner diversity, the ability to exploit new
niches, new opportunities.

For our seed to flourish we must nurture the
germ at its core—the open
heart and the open door; the germ of the open,
loving spirit.
This is the spirit that creates communities
for meeting human need, free from the
narrowing creed, the rigid ideology, the
oppressive institution.

Our seed, when truly rich in the values we
affirm, will root and grow—yielding harvests
for the human spirit and the world's wholeness.

Clifford M. Reed
*United Kingdom*

# Remembrance

Eternal God,
in whose ways lie the destiny of all peoples,
We remember before thee
the heroism of men and the fortitude of women
in times of trial:
Those who endured with valour
and suffered in patience;
Those who gave all that they had or hoped to be
in anticipation of a better world.
And we remember the folly and the errors,
the unhallowed ambitions
of nations and leaders,
which so wastefully committed the ordinary and the brave
to the horrors and bereavements of war.

Fill again the hearts and wills of all people of this globe
with love and loyalty to each other and to thee.
Give harmony to the councils of all nations
and of all concerned with international goodwill;
Give unity of purpose to all who work for peace.
Make all men and women to seek and live for
universal understanding and friendship;

and help us to establish over all the earth
thy kingdom of righteousness and love.
Amen.

Sydney H. Knight
*United Kingdom*

# Prayer for an Interfaith Gathering

Almighty God of Grace, who has spared us to see the blessing of this great day added to our unlimited grace, and who has been pleased to bind us together in order to think, deliberate, and partake in love, peace, and happiness as men and women of various languages and creeds throughout the Universe:

As you have given us this grace, our thoughts are different, our behaviour various, yet we thank Thee Lord. Let us be more united in Spirit and in deed that we may be thine in grace, happiness, and development.

Let us have the mind to help each other in all our days, in order to show our belief, as true lovers of religious freedom.

We remember now our sisters and brothers around the world. Protect them that all may live in safety.

We ask these things in Thy Holy Name, our Creator, our Great Leader and Ruler of the Universe.

The Unitarian Brotherhood Church
*Nigeria*

adapted

# To Live Means to Live Together

The basis of our ideas rests on agreement rather than revelation. Our starting point is each person's religious beliefs.

In a process of communication and mutual understanding, we seek to articulate our common views. In the spirit of freedom, each member's religious conviction is respected.

Although our basic ideas have much to do with critical reasoning, we acknowledge also that there is an emotional side to human experience.

All religious contemplation refers to beginnings; the evolution of life and the universe and the place of human beings in it. We are aware of the constant changes in the world and in our conceptions of it. As human consciousness has changed before, so it will change again.

Human beings are woven into the web of nature. We may feel at home there. In our festivals we follow the seasons of nature and of human life.

For any system to flourish it must have variety. We acknowledge the variety of human life and seek its enlargement, affirming the power of tolerance over fundamentalism, the worth of the individual over totalitarianism.

As human beings, capable of both love and destruction, we acknowledge that living in society sometimes requires of us the renunciation of our claims and influence. Aware of our interdependence, we understand the world about us as both ours and everyone else's.

Human life develops best in the peaceful co-habitation of responsible people. We would contribute actively to this aim in our own society and country and as part of humankind.

We would seek for the peaceful resolution of conflicts by means of understanding, but acknowledge that there are conflicts which we cannot resolve. These we must endure.

We live in nature and are part of it. We feel our obligation to treat it with respect, even if personal sacrifices are required.

To live means to live together.

Helmut Kramer, translated by Manfred J. Paul

*Germany*

# We Believe

We believe that the mountains and valleys,
the sorrows and joys of life,
cannot be confined to formulae or dogma;
That humankind is a mystery—
open and questioning.
We have no sure answers to the basic questions of life,
but we have faith in the existence of a universal God-Power,
which can be envisioned in many different ways—
And we assume that all religions spring from this same source.

Let us pray, and work for the day when
    we all may live in harmony with our environment.
That we, and all of humanity,
    may learn to live in peace,
And that we may nourish and develop our understanding,
    of both our neighbours and ourselves.
    Amen.

Anonymous, translated by Lene Lund Shoemaker
*Denmark*

# Longing for Harmony

In the name of Providence, which implants in the seed the future of the flower, and in our hearts the longing for people to live in harmony;

In the name of the highest, in whom we move and who makes the mother and father, the brother and sister, lover and loner what they are;

In the name of sages and great religious leaders, who sacrificed their lives to hasten the coming of the age of mutual respect;

Let us renew our resolution—sincerely to be real brothers and sisters regardless of any kind of bar which estranges us from each other.

In this holy resolve may we be strengthened, knowing that we are God's family; that one spirit, the spirit of love, unites us;

and endeavour for a more perfect and more joyful life.

Norbert Capek
*Czech Republic*

# Roads

I enjoy looking at other people's roads.
They are different from mine
and yet basically the same.
They all facilitate journey
from here to there,
from self to other,
and they are all interconnected.

The fact that I love my own road
with its comfortable landmarks
and familiar faces,
doesn't restrict my appreciation
of someone else's neighbourhood.

And if I go into another area
and walk a mile or two with someone else,
I return as a larger being.
The love of my own road is deepened,
the appreciation of other roads is widened,
and I am blessed in the knowledge
that all roads lead to God.

Joy Cowley
*New Zealand*

# About the International Council of Unitarians and Universalists

At the 1987 Annual Meeting of the General Assembly of British Unitarian and Free Christian Churches, the following resolution was passed almost unanimously:

> That this General Assembly..., in glad recognition of the presence of Unitarianism in twenty countries and on five continents, requests the General Assembly Council to consult with Unitarian representatives throughout the world and explore the possibility of establishing a World Unitarian Council.

The main goals in the formation of such a World Council were, among others:

- to promote cooperation between Unitarians and Universalists around the world for the enhancement of existing national organizations,
- to establish and foster a new presence in countries that lack a Unitarian presence without the danger of a single organization assuming that task alone,
- to support small Unitarian groups not yet able to be self-sufficient, and
- to generate awareness of Unitarianism [Universalism] as a world faith.

As a result, an organization was formed under the peculiar name of "Advocates for the Establishment of an International Organization of Unitarians" (AEIOU). The coordinator and spokesman of the group was Rev. David Usher, a British Unitarian minister of Australian origin and a fundamental figure in the formation, establishment, and consolidation of ICUU.

From March 23 through March 26, 1995, representatives of Unitarian and Unitarian Universalist congregations from the United States, Europe, Canada, South Africa, Philippines, Sri Lanka, Australia, and New Zealand gathered in Essex, Massachusetts (USA), to establish the Principles and Bylaws of the International Council of Unitarians and Universalists, which now read,

> We, the member groups of the International Council of
> Unitarians and Universalists, affirming our belief in religious
> community based on:
>> liberty of conscience and individual thought in matters
>> of faith,
>> the inherent worth and dignity of every person.
>> justice and compassion in human relations,
>> responsible stewardship in human relations,
>> and our commitment to democratic principles,
> declare our purposes to be:
>> to serve the Infinite Spirit of Life and the human community
>> by strengthening the worldwide Unitarian and Universalist
>> faith,
>> to affirm the variety and richness of our living traditions,
>> to facilitate mutual support among member organizations,

to promote our ideals and principles around the world,
to provide models of liberal religious response to the human
condition which upholds our common values.

The current membership of ICUU is as follows:

*Full Membership:*

Australian and New Zealand Unitarian Association
Canadian Unitarian Council
The Religious Society of Czech Unitarians
Unitarisk Kirksamfund of Denmark
European Unitarian Universalists
Deutsche Unitarier Religionsgemeinschaft (Germany)
General Assembly of Unitarian and Free Christian Churches
    (United Kingdom)
The Unitarian Church of Hungary
Indian Council of Unitarian Churches
Unitarian Brotherhood Church of Nigeria
Unitarian Universalist Church of Pakistan
Unitarian Universalist Church of the Philippines
The Unitarian Church in Poland
The Unitarian Church of Romania (Transylvania)
Moscow Unitarian Advocates (Russia)
Unitarian Church of South Africa
Unitarian Universalist Association of Sri Lanka
Unitarian Universalist Association of Congregations (United
    States)

*Associate Membership:*

The Unitarian Christian Association of Northern Ireland

*Provisional Membership:*

Unitarian Fellowship of Finland
Sociedad Unitaria Universalista de Espana (Spain)
First Unitarian Universalist Church of Ghana

*Emerging Groups:*

Argentina
Brazil
Bolivia
Latvia

# Notes on Contributors

NORBERT CAPEK—Czech Unitarian minister, founder of Czech Unitarian movement. Died in a Nazi concentration camp in 1942.

CLIFFORD M. REED—British Unitarian minister, former president of the British General Assembly, and the first secretary of ICUU.

JOY COWLEY—New Zealand poet and hymn writer.

SHEILA CROSSKEY—active British Unitarian layperson with interest in Third World development.

JAUME DE MARCOS—Spanish-born active Unitarian Universalist layperson and member of European Unitarian Universalists. A professional translator.

SAMINA TUFAIL GILL—Active and committed contact person with the scattered Unitarian Universalists of Pakistan.

V. EMIL GUDMUNDSON—Served as a district executive for the Prairie Star District of the Unitarian Universalist Association in the United States. Held an honorary doctor of divinity degree from Meadville Lombard Theological School. Died in 1982.

GYÖRGY ANDRÁSI—Romanian Unitarian minister serving in Transylvania.

KAREL HASPL—Czech Unitarian minister who served as a successor to Norbert Capek. Died in 1964.

CHRISTINA JONES—Northern Irish schoolteacher and poet.

JOZSEF K. KASZONI—Romanian Unitarian minister who has served in Transylvania and Budapest in Hungary.

SYDNEY KNIGHT—Retired British Unitarian minister, hymn writer, and hymnal editor.

HELMUT KRAMER—Leading member of Deutche Unitarier, Germany.

MANFRED J. PAUL—Leading member of Deutche Unitarier, Germany.

JAMES MARTINEAU—Unitarian minister, academic, and hymn writer. He died in 1900.

LEONARD MASON—British-born Unitarian minister who served in the United

Kingdom and Canada. Minister emeritus of the Unitarian Church of Montreal in Quebec. He died in 1995.

MAURY MERKIN—A member of Cedar Lane Unitarian Universalist Church in Bethesda, Maryland, for nearly twenty years.

ANGUS M. McCORMICK—Northern Irish Unitarian minister who has served in England and Northern Ireland.

JOHN MIDGLEY—British Unitarian minister. President of the British General Assembly, 2001-2002.

JOAN MONTAGNES—Canadian Unitarian Universalist minister presently serving in Idaho, United States.

SHIRLEY MURRAY—New Zealand poet and hymn writer.

ELEK REZI—Unitarian minister, deputy bishop of the Unitarian Church of Romania.

LENE LUND SHOEMAKER—Vice president and international relations co-ordinator of the Unitarian Church of Copenhagen in Denmark.

PERE CARL Q. SIENES—Moderator of the Unitarian Universalist Church of the Philippines.

REBECCA Q. SIENES—Unitarian Universalist minister and president of the Unitarian Universalist Church of the Philippines.

ROBERT STEYN—South African Unitarian minister who served in Capetown and died in 1997.

JOHN ANDREW STOREY—British Unitarian minister and prolific hymn writer who died in 1997.

MIKLOS SZÉKELY—Romanian Unitarian minister serving in Transylvania.

ELSPETH R. VALLANCE—Retired British Unitarian minister now living in New Zealand.

ROBERT T. WESTON—American Unitarian minister. Served First Unitarian Church of Louisville, Kentucky, in the 1950s.